…aggressive

ISBN-13: 978-0-9996018-2-2 (Innate Divinity)
ISBN-10: 0999601822

Cover Design: Eric DeVaughnn

…aggressive

Eric DeVaughnn
T.R.U.E

INNATE DIVINITY
San Bernardino/Houston

I dedicate this book to every officer who ever took aim at me, every sales associate who ever followed me around a store, every church I ever loved and left, every coworker who felt threatened by my quiet, my hoodie, my blank face; to my former faith, my new peace; to each ex for my brokenness, my foolishness, my wisdom, my hope; to every laugh, to every heartache, to every private hell, every joyous occasion; to everything that has made me who I am, and to the unfortunate conversation which became the inspiration for the title poem [if I'm aggressive when choosing to walk away from conflict, when am I not?]

To each of the fallen brothers and sisters acknowledged in this text and those left unsaid who, too soon, have transitioned to the ancestors; may you ever rest in power.

And to every man, woman, or child who knows what it is to be unjustly called, viewed as, or treated like you are aggressive,

I see you.

Love you Mom.

Love you Grandma.
Janie Mikele, this is for you.

(Rosalie, you're next)

That, by which you define yourself most proudly, will always be that, on which you will work most fervently.

T. R. U. E

CAUTION:

May Contain Broken Shards and Pointed Edges. Not Suitable for Small Children. Adult Supervision is Advised.

table of contents

poem:

Treasonous

we walk in days
when black
life is defiance
so with every treasonous
breath
I speak against injustice
to tear down
a system
never
meant

for me

we | CREATED | life I listen with intent | wrists bent in a fashion not meant for my people | our natural passion forever unequaled | see, we CREATED life | and I'm just excited to learn | the curiosity of a child's mind | so full of queries and theories | and with the prospect of knowledge so near me | you stifle it with "sit down! be quiet!" | so, hidden | I sit here | cloaked in melanin | while those of fairer skin attempt to tell me where I've been | yet conveniently omit that egypt is really kemet | so I forget that I come from pharoahs' kin | made of the very same element up from which god brought the earth | I sit here and I learn what you think

my thoughts are worth

WE | created | life I listen with intent | wrists bent in a fashion not meant for my people | our natural passion forever unequaled | see, WE created life | and the power of our voice cannot be contained | so take no offense to the resonance of god | rumbling though my chest | the residence of god | whether or not I speak | I speak and cannot be silent | and with the prospect of progress so near | me you stifle it with "fuck your breath!" | so hated | I sit here | clothed in melanin | armed for destruction in the truest sense | but you don't fear me | this critical chemical in my complexion is a reflection of the direct threat to your very existence | and so at your insistence | I make no attempt to reason against your leveled weapon's persistence | against instruction meant to prevent corruption | when I show no intention of obstruction | and though I love the burnt brass cast of this | my earthen vessel | I'm wrestled down like I made the choice at birth | I sit here and I learn what you think

my voice is worth

we | created | LIFE

I listen with intent | wrists bent in a fashion not meant for my people | our natural passion forever unequaled | see, we created LIFE | and ironically | you attempted to give it back to me twice | LIFE you declared with cold eyes | as my new truth gave way to old lies | LIFE I stand here old, wise | yet still in shackles while you apologize | LIFE exonerated "now back to your hood, boy" | LIFE while the church folk cry | "god is so good!" boy, I tell ya the game is too cold | how you offer me a second chance when it was you who stole | so, humbly | I sit here | robed in melanin | as you measure out the days I listen in a daze | only vaguely aware of the time you gave me | but gravely aware of the time you took | time the children I won't teach | time the communities I won't reach | time my kids will never see | time my mother misses me | time my brothers needed me | but time has not defeated me | an absent king | my joy my queen | my soul | my wife was hurt | I sit here and I learn how much you think

my LIFE is worth

My Street

I grew up on a quiet street
trees   lined the   yards
ever-shaded   pavement
beginning with the
patient   curve
                    at block's end

here   in my today
all these many years later
I live on a street like that
                                again

no curve at one end
but I can walk   and
smile with the trees

it feels, once   more
        like   Home

Caliber

for some reason
I keep putting myself
in hopeless situations

de li ber ate ly

almost like I'm trying
to gauge
the caliber of Man
I really am

Is, the truth is not

Is subjective

despite how they heard it

don't care how you word it is is

and just how absurd it must

seem at the time to assume

that opinion can be above blame

so beyond reproach faultless and

true when reality this, what is simply is

deny my eye dispute my ear

defy my presence my

knowledge my being to try

just how valid is

all that I know

will not refute the existence of e x is t e n c e

permanence cannot be debated

so beyond reproach faultless and

true reality, this your lies amiss

for all that you do what is simply is

Man   on

he had life

I don't know that he had a home but

he displayed a friendly and warm, engaging Smile

an energy that could displace any sense of negativity

his sign was the best part:

"please Help. mentally eclectic. will spit similes, imagery,
and metaphor Food"

every day

I'd drive past the same place I'd seen the

same man standing again in the same spot

every day lifting his message

Truth is in him I see too much of myself

at once a rebellious spirit masking many insecurities and

I wonder what made my world heave and thrust vomit

him into this receptacle assign him a New

place in life He, resigned to feeble and commit to this

less than ethical truce abuse of power

reduced his righteous voice crying in the wilderness

to three lines scribbled on a cardboard sign:

the   Corner

"please Help. mentally eclectic. will spit similes, imagery, and metaphor Food"

without

understanding his path if only

to avoid taking it home and

making it my own I'd rather turn my head

in the other direction focused intently on my

internal reflection hoping he sees

how busy I am and doesn't bother me for the

loose change

commingling with the lint in my pocket Gathering dust in my seat

settling in the rust round my feet

one day he simply wasn't there

another had rotated into his spot completely devoid of the genuine

Joy he'd brought realizing how Important he'd become to

me, I sought him and after some weeks

found him resting on the outskirts of a local public park

stark contrast to his previous location giant shade

trees now inviting Offered to envelope him with

Patient arms

when I noticed how the patrons armed themselves with
indignation possessed the park would not let him near it to
heal his wounded spirit
I saw in them too much of myself
so now
I stop by every once and often time
to sit with him beneath the trees Offer him
a Smile of my own beneath branches and leaves
bent and swayed like healing hands offers to help him find
his way call his spirit
back to living lands
I watch them try and revive it watch them administer cc's of
adrenaline in hopes his weak pulse will survive it
allow my mind to drift back to the place we'd met
hanging along the very edge foot forward into the perfect
wedge where I now in turn spit similes, imagery, and
Metaphor Food and perform like the

former builder rejected stone on this
curb intersected
reminiscent of the man I met

on the corner

In Which I Do Not Apologize to the Roach for the Spray

[audio]

I happen to catch
your reflection in the mirror
on the bathroom wall
of the house
into which
I have just moved

your feeble attempt to hide
leads me to believe
you don't fully comprehend
the futility
of your inaction
nor I
the beauty bold
of contrasting color

you
glossy brown-backed black
stand out too well
off against white floors
you do not sufficiently blend

with paint flecks beige
soft cream tile
snowy countertop
really
any member of
family "fair"

so I see you

your presence suddenly
a most unwelcome
interruption

of my spotless view

and while, you were here
lo n g
before
I ever

you have been appropriately

g e n t r i f i e d

I cannot apologize for your life

your breath*is mild nuisance
so it only fair
my spit* contain just enough venom
each fateful droplet
glistening with the perspiration of

murderous work*
carried out in sentences*
never spoken
*often*said
go back where you come from

*or lie on the ground

*gasping

until this*poison*in my mouth*
kills me *slow* enough
to watch *you* die

* * *first

I Used to Fly

walking out to lunch I noticed a crow
pecking at the district office lawn
I initially held it as simply a reference point
to avoid watching the triad of booties directly ahead
yes ladies it takes a concentrated effort not to stare

gradually I became interested in whatever had so captured
the bird's attention and watched as it pulled something out of
the soil It looked around and
with quick bounce flew off just a few feet above the street

for the briefest moment I felt a sense of wonderment reminiscent
to the curiosity and creativity I had
as a little boy that allowed me to experience flight
through the power of imagination
and I smiled
in that second I was at peace

many years removed from childlike wonder I don't fly anymore
when becoming adult it's easy to lose sight of the simple
moments that brought you such joy and freedom in your youth
but every once in a while it's nice to visit

Local Eric Translation

1 Stand fast therefore in the liberty wherewith Christ hath made you
free, and be not entangled again with the yoke of bondage. 2 Unless
you're into that sort of thing. *

Galatians 5:1-2 (L E T)

*contains some shit from the king james bible

Lies

of the people
by the people
for the people*

was given
to the people

*contains some shit from the gettysburg address

RANDOM THOUGHT

"but when I became a Man..."

Interesting how perspectives change throughout life.

As a child, I was deathly afraid that I would die in quicksand. I also wanted to be a cop so I could shoot people.

Now that I'm grown, I see how ridiculous one of these ideas was.

A few years ago, I was playing paintball with four friends in a burned out, abandoned house on a few acres of secluded property. As I got the drop on my opponents, they suddenly looked past me, dropped their paintball markers, and raised their hands.

"Uh, Chief? I really think you should put that down..."
I thought they were trying to trick me into looking, but indeed, there was an officer behind me, weapon drawn.

As we sat along the wall at gunpoint, waiting for his backup, we answered questions and had a pleasant enough conversation - muzzle notwithstanding.

When six cars arrived, sirens blaring, I listened to the disappointed officers telling each other how much they were looking forward to this call:

"Man, I thought I was gonna get to shoot somebody!"

"At least the drive was fun!"

Then, they picked up the paintball markers we'd dropped and started playing with them, shooting them off, while we sat in cuffs a full 40 min after they were satisfied no crime had taken place, my paperwork verified, background check clear.

That wasn't the first time the police had pointed a loaded gun at me for no reason.

But I've still never even seen quicksand.

Growing Up Apostolic

although I learned
to fear the rapture

my soul at stake
in heavenly hands

dealt, played
by demon and divine

seated 'round
felt-lined tables
in velvet galaxies;

it was my father
who taught me

most effective
that people can
disappear
for reasons
far less
m y s t i c a l

My Locs

my locs grow inward
tangled and intertwined
permeating the spaces of my righteous
free mind   these days I find
my entire consciousness turned on end
so that each twist extends
upward to greet the eternal force,
this internal sun   one and only
illuminating source
my guiding light
brighter than   blinding brights
tap tap, roll it down show me some
ID   friday night's

identify me quickly
before I find my
identity

all the while within

dread the shedding of loose fears and rejection's tears
a broken soul made manifest wholly by healing hands,
older than Miyagi Palm roll
my evolution is
this inner conflict:
peace and hope now interlocked with my intellect
intersected with institutional confusion meets
revolution and introspect

so now
inwardly, my locs, they grow
tapping into the ethereal spring
of life water flow
drink long gulps take deep cleansing breath
turn CO2 into precious drafts of featherweight molecules
to float away on the weightless whispers of a sensuous breeze
these tendrils are leaves
simultaneously bearing fruits
while exhaling life up into my sky
pulling essential nutrients
from the hue-man experience
like squeezing rich black motherland soil
between each bare toe

I proudly display this
spirit new growth
questing ever onward for knowledge
seeking to sate this thirst, his
speaking relates in verses
fueled by formless food
my unseen antennae protrude, like
here, feed the lyrical atmosphere
and connect with this
empirical data drawn
from the strata's dawn
and spawn anew

my locs grow on the inside
look closely and listen
you'll see 'em pushing through

my locs

Weapons of Warfare * [audio]

"for the weapons of our warfare are not carnal but mighty though god to the pulling down of strongholds"

(we sit in buildings wielding the word as a weapon)

"wrestle not against flesh and blood"
"who can separate us from his love"

(sold and separated, ripped from flesh and blood)

Words as weapons:

- "turn the other cheek"
- "blessed are the meek"
- "when I am weak, then am I made strong"
- "if in this life only we have hope, we are of all men most miserable"
- "but I go to prepare a place that where I am, you may be also"

"for I reckon that the sufferings of this present time are not worthy to be compared with the glory that shall be revealed in us"

*contains some shit from the king james bible

After America Determines Beyoncé to be Black and Kendrick Lamar Too Much Out Loud

[video]

I'm tired of smiling
attempting to correct your hateful rebuttal
respectfully deflecting your not-quite-so-subtle ignorance patiently
expounding upon simple ideas to simple minds teaching critical
thinking to brick walls

reaching to save the few last jewels of uncommon sense from
spilling through the cracks of a broken intellect
you are my constant reminder that
thought requires uncommon effort
try harder

and what do you know of my culture anyway
Beyoncé whatever urban music your grandchildren
Kendrick you into listening to if you halftime Grammy

you'll have to excuse my tone
I was raised to respect my elders
but no one taught my parents how to honor the ancestors

White Sheets

upon which he was conceived
wrinkles and crevice molded
conformed to deep brown thighs
swirling about the natural chaos of passions ebony flow
awash in flooded spots broken and watery
twisted in adrenaline upon which she did labor and bring him to
LIFE

within which he was swaddled
carefully wrapped a gift patiently prepared
his first voice a pinprick into the wind
a sour call mourning   wailed in protest
how he would foreshadow the hopelessness to come
and with this did a newborn cry
pepper sterile halls and litter the very sky

into which he was placed
tucked to chin on a bed of coiled spring
vertical bars foretold the future his country meant to bring

under which he slaved the day away to build a makeshift tent
coincidentally between two poplar trees
he smiled and braved the elements

through which he ran to hide and seek out
streams of broken sunlight's beams
clipped to lines like flags of peace
dancing in the gentle breeze

from which a mother sought to keep his innocence corrupted
the timelessness of horses hooves on dusted streets erupted

a rhythm beat in angry ears
as vivid pictures stepped through years
to claim her soul in frantic fears
and poison memories

pointed ghost of childhood hosting
flames upon her home   but
by her soul it would not be
visited on her own

throughout which by threaded count
a single weave could represent
each single darkened LIFE at sea
from liquid grave to pavement

from trees to cross the loved ones lost to centuries of woe
she swore upon the ancestors her son would never know

beneath which lay a bloody form
a man unjustly slain
he'd seen the bullets pierce the air and
heard the screams of pain

impressed on with desire
to lift up and inquire
if it was indeed himself beneath that chaste and holy thing
but as he reached a trembling hand
to see a face that should not be
his spirit did ascend upon these well and weathered wing

over which he lifted pen for record of his deeds
no ink would flow and thus would end his life

with blank white sheets

Local Eric Translation

2 And the angel of the Lord appeared unto him in a flame of fire out of the midst of a bush: and he looked, and behold, the bush burned with fire, and the bush was not consumed. 3 And Moses said, Not sure why, but suddenly I have the munchies... *

Exodus 3:2-3 (LET)

*contains some shit from the king james bible

Torturous

eyes
dancing
somber samba
hopelessly pulled
into dual infinity
pools
of serenity
your depths
are become
muse to
fuse divinity
your
cocoa
chokehold
already has me

I could live
f o r e v e r
in this *CURVE*

just…
lightly…
breathing…
slightly...
your
prickle
flesh
whisper
secrets
back
to
me
and
I haven't
even
TOUCHED
you
yet

if I ever leave California

I will miss the one thing I cannot take with me

In-and-Out

number one, extra pickles, no onions, with a pink lemonade.

I say no onions, but truth is I like the flavor on the burger

just without the actual onion

I like chopping them

peeling back   layers

smell   in my fingers

from separating rings

but the   bitterness

left behind   to linger   in my mouth

sharply nips at buds   on my tongue

              like trying to pet a stray dog

wandering through   dim   lit   streets

wary of affection

or a loved one

with no direction

trying to replace the family

he thought had abandoned him
        or she   seeking home
        far away from her own
craving attention and empathy

bitter to the palate
makes it difficult to reach   out
when they bite   at your   love

these are the onions

if ever around
they add flavor to the room
broken smiles which never quite seem
to crack the corners of eyes

I have such a brother

when infrequently I see him
I can never quite remember
to

                Hold the Onions

RANDOM THOUGHT

"super sick"

Just realized something:

When I'm sick at work, my professional mask changes significantly. No longer does mild-mannered professional educator, Eric D. Thompson transform into P.E. Guy Extraordinaire to use his powers for good; for even he has fallen prey to the whims of his dark alter ego...

SuperDGAFman.

Special powers/abilities:

- Can stop a child cold in his tracks with his icy "Imminent Death" Gaze
- Can silently curse people out from his very soul

ArchNemesis:

As an alternate personality, SuperDGAFman possesses the body of P.E. Guy Extraordinaire.

Motivation:

Believes everyone is stupid and must be destroyed

Fatal flaw:

- Crippling cognitive dissonance
- Consumed by burning impulsiveness juxtaposed with a brazen superiority complex
- Grew up Apostolic

Catch-phrase:

"Hey, real talk? I SUPER dgaf."

Hm...

Anybody else wonder how that story turns out?

Because I think I just found my next graphic novel.

welcome | The Protector

welcome into the mind of a mild mannered alter ego | this predominately pleasant and patiently peaceful pe teacher | features mild manners | altered negro | for the sake of my secret identity I can only say so much | but for nearly 20 years I have quietly dawned the daily mantle of adoptive father | called daddy by babies not of my bloodline | born to countless mothers whom I never knew | it was exciting in the beginning

rushing into burning buildings | a human torch igniting and lighting up young minds | a one-man infantry | hellboy at war with a broken system | hell-bent on choking wisdom in its vital infancy | racing off in a flash to save the weak from dangers unseen by | doctors, strangers | and each unique child born with mystique the | uncanny ability to look just like me | who am I? I'm black man | apparently an unlikely source of defense | or so the story goes | so the story is told repeated and sold|boldly amended for names and changes in locations but for all my frustrations | I battle this nemesis | contending with lack of appreciation | pretending it doesn't hurt when | bullets intended for children | bounce off my chest and burn like | tears bourn on the mourning of a thousand sons | when one thousand daughters cry | and wonder when their salvation comes | that's when I at the speed of light I run | fly mach 5 from the moment of my takeoff | ready to take off this shirt | and take off on somebody trying to get hurt | when the world | when the world piles on my kids | I take it upon me and lift up with immeasurable strength | shake off negative perceptions of men | when there are so many more like me doing all that we can

and though we rarely show it | it takes its toll consistently doing right in the face of wrong | so I'll continue to fight | press against the horde | if need be driven by pure will for no reward | see this | this must be how superheroes feel | when they say | "because if I don't | who will?"

you and I
were never more than the sum of broken promises

happy lies
balanced on the tips of dark and lonely smiles

all the while we   the happy two
planting strange kisses with the seed of stolen fruit
hung from forked tongue   truth unspoken became spoken
untruth whispered and sung in the grooves of deceptive lips
          when planting   strange kisses

Happy Lies:

stranger still
we were strangely familiar   strangers
familiar with copious means of keeping up appearances
when neither of us even knew what   copious means
                    or love really

ours was either a sultry glance
or the beautiful dance of shadows cast by crooked and frail forest

[audio]

naked trees

balding branches bent to infidelity

backlit by

flames of infatuation who lick at the nubile night

and reach Reach for the deception of stars

trapped in the bold void upon which we faithfully spoke dictations

and daily affirmations your independent persuasions were

dismissed with every word I uttered

gems fluttered away and pinned upon a cluttered missive

The Married Woman

but dammit if we didn't look good

matching tones blend like voices played in unison like

choices made in unison this lunacy the illusion of unity

like your curves were meant for me Like these words

were meant to be spoken in pleasure

but

over the measure of our days together

I finally came to realize it was purely by coincidence

that we ever played the same note in the chorus

of two different melodies

Woman

one of these days you
are going to realize the
w i s d o m
in s i m p l e words

like

"Le t i t G O"

Upon Measures

religion is in itself
a system of control
mass conformity
heaping measure upon
m e a s u r e
precept upon precept
without these systems
would society crumble?
did we create god to
e x p l a i n
what we don't know?

Mom's Cornbread

1 cup cornmeal

1 cup flour

1 tbsp baking powder

1|2 tsp salt

1|2 cup sugar

1 whole egg

1 cup milk

1|2 cup butter-flavored Crisco

preheat oven

mix dry ingredients first

beat an egg in the corner

stir in milk until mixture is wet

melt butter-flavored Crisco

pour in the batter and bake at

450deg for 20-25min

I love my mother's cornbread.

But it was difficult when I realized she wouldn't always be here to make it. So I followed my mom around the kitchen for that recipe. A grown man in my 30's I followed, taking notes of verbal quotes because she had never bothered to write it down. She was so familiar with the process that it had become part of her.

As I watched her rattle off ingredients, intrigued by her effortless flow, dancing with the dish she'd prepared for me countless times, I couldn't help but wonder about the first...

How did she know what to do?

Were there times when she knew she didn't whip it enough and just had to take the lumps?

Did she ever spoil the batch with too much sugar? Use baking soda instead of baking powder?

I stood in that kitchen, the first of four increasingly difficult sons. I, the untested recipe she hoped would come out ok; the unproven dish over which she'd pored and prayed; into which she had mixed both smiles and tears, poured cups of love, stirred in affection, beat discipline into the corners of a rapidly developing young black male ego.

We'd go back and forth over the years,
and I'm sure I could've been a better son...

I am dichotomous.

Sometimes the spitting image of the broken man who damaged her trust, reflecting his mannerisms all too familiar. And sometimes, I am the dark and masculine picture she sees when she smiles at the face in her own mirror.

And although I tend toward gentleman, a sinner, a cynic, a scholar; occasionally, I can't help but wonder:

How did she know what to do?

Were there times when she knew she didn't whip me enough and just had to take her lumps?

I wondered whether I ever caused her regret...
On my 35th birthday, she answered and quieted that thought with this text:

"Happy Birthday to my first born! Your father and I were in the trailer park talking and my labor pains started. We went to the hospital on base. The doc checked me and said it would be at least 6 hours. Everyone left - the doctor, your dad. My bp was up and I was shaking because of the pain but you didn't care what the doc said. You were ready. 30 minutes later around 5 you were here! 5 lbs 6 ozs I think and most beautiful baby ever! I've loved you ever since. Enjoy your day!"

Lately I've been in the kitchen. Tentatively exploring my own recipe. Gathered ingredients, preheated the oven to late November, warming my hands over smoldering stove embers.

I'm proud to have my mother, my example around to sample my first batch. And in the coming years when fears and doubt threaten to consume my head, I'll pull up her text, smile, and recall I was Mom's first recipe for cornbread.

RANDOM THOUGHT

I figure this one is going to disappoint a few of you.
Oh well. *Pray for me.*

I have known many people in my life, most of whom are Christian. Some of them believe that prayer has been removed from schools. Of that group, some feel that if prayer had not been removed from schools, then there would be fewer school shootings.

First, gun legislation has more to do with the abundance of school shootings, church shootings, theater shootings, Vegas shootings, club shootings, and sorority house shootings than anything else - including prayer. If the weapon is not so readily available, then the potential for mass shootings is drastically reduced. Why can't we use the same logic that went into the changes in airport security? Someone tried the system with a shoe bomb once and now we all take off our shoes? Someone shoots at a crowd of people every few months and nothing changes? Why should we have to convince the government to do something about it, especially when gun lobbies already argue on behalf of their product reaching as many people as possible?

Second, prayer has NOT been removed from schools. Government-sanctioned and school-mandated prayer have been removed. That simply means the government says (and rightly so) it is not the school's place to require everyone to pray. However, individuals cannot be prohibited from expressing religious thoughts, as they are deemed free speech. Students can pray. Teachers can pray. My high school had a Christian club. I've worked at schools that hold regular bible classes for staff members who want to join. Prayer isn't gone.

Lastly, calling for more religious freedom won't do anything to help, because that particular freedom is not being infringed upon. It is alive and well.

What WILL help is changing how easily shooters access the weapons they use. What WILL make a difference is taking away the powerful lobby, and its ability to pressure the government to further the cause for private financial interests. What WILL work is changing the gun culture in America. Don't blame it on prayer. Don't just think happy thoughts. DO something. CHANGE THE SYSTEM. If you want something else to pray for, pray for that. Then, get up and vote because Washington doesn't respond to prayers.

You know...separation of church and state and all...

The 1st Wednesday after
The 1st Tuesday after
The 1st Monday November 2016

I don't understand this at all

The sun still shining sky, blue as has ever been
rolling mountains laugh in gleeful abandon while I
am stoic

children run and play smiling full and bright
blissfully unaware of impending nightmares
set in motion

somehow, the earth spins without tilting off center
off her charted course sent careening into the sun

who, amid the very end
of life as we know it would probably still shine

Dreaming of an Ex

how many

times

must I

brutally m u r d e r

the g h o s t of

your memory

before

you l earn

to s t a y

g o n e ?

Left Unsaid

You don't know it but, I still watch you...

I've seen you out, running your errands, or sometimes just driving down the street. I'm sure you didn't know I was there because you never even turned in my general direction. I've even seen you sleeping, curled up against the new "best thing to ever happen to you."

Yes, it hurts me that you left me to pursue someone else. And for what? No one will ever love you like I did…and still do. And always will. You'll never find anyone who can do for you what I can, be to you what I can be.

You have to admit it – if you recall, you were better for having known me. Even when things were rough, you used to come to me and let me be strong for you. When you didn't need me anymore, I recognized. And when you started to pull away, it hurt but I had to let you go.

You know…the hardest thing for me to accept is that, even though we aren't together anymore, you know that I'm right for you. And you still don't get it:
I'm here.

I've been ever since you walked away. And all it would take to win me back is to open up your heart to what you know to be true.

Please don't be mistaken – I'm going to be just fine without you if you decide you never want me back. But I do love you. You couldn't possibly understand just how much. If you won't let me save you from yourself, then just know this - no matter what you do, where you go, how far you run, I will always be your Creator.

If not your God.

Local Eric Translation

3 And I heard the voice of the Lord speak unto me, saying 4 Son of
man, why is thine visage darkened and why is thine countenance
wroth? 5 And I answered and said, It's these niggas, Lord…it's all
these niggas. 6 And then was the visage of the Lord darkened and
His countenance wroth, because of the niggas.

B ackSl id er

"I N TH E
W O R L D
BU T NO T
O F I T"

Well I'm of it cuz I'm in it
And love it cuz a minute
ago I was so independently
sold in the ministry Told
I could enter in
boldy the throne
now
I'm only alone and unholy

I'm coming back

"...aggressive" [video]

I'm sorry
I almost loved you
almost let the home we started to build together
negate the worlds of distance between us

cha sms grand and ever-w i dening
like the candied sweet toothy smiles
you always laid on my pillow

what I wouldn't give to smile like *that*
what I would not give to bare my *teeth* and
be no beast wild
be no burden of
civilized man whipped and tamed into
silent and civil unrest

what I wouldn't give willingly
just so it could not be taken

you wanted me to accept
the things you hold dear
even when they hurt

that's just how they are

but you cannot accept the thing in me
that screams in protest
you criticize my revolutionary bones
but

that's just how they are

when I walk like a King
purposeful and dignified
you want me to apologize
for each and every
AGGRESSIVE step

you watch me
hunt for shade
prowl for rest

a peaceful predator
you prey
on my trust

but my soul is a   domesticated thing
returning to   wilderness
subsaharan desert plains
and jungles deep
call me   home
call me   blessed for this
crown you have   cursed

when I run   there must be   some crime
some grave sin   just around the corner
surely justice is only steps behind

as you imagine   carnage in my wake

you jog on   pushing soft through gentle
winds

what I wouldn't give to *run* like that
what I would not give to
FLY FREE and be no   great and pouncing cat
no   sprinting lion
no   terrible bundle of claws
coiled to *spring* on you   every time
every time?   *I almost loved you*

I didn't know
you still see me as
ravenous embrace
a warm and cozy
feast of flesh,
ripped and pulled
from the folds
of your tender belly
monster in mitten hands

I can no longer recall
exactly when
but it seems I am become
blood-soaked grin
in place of careful and
tight-lipped smile

and you

you have learned to love
my thick padded paws best
when they tiptoe
around *your pride*

aggressive

Woman You More

I don't sleep
not like I used to

I no longer dream
of pulling you close
pushing my thoughts
deep into the crux
where your thighs
meet heart

you
straddle me depth
these hands
seek nothing but
to woman you more

buttons unclasp
collarbone to supple slow
handlebar your waist
you ride my waves
we passion deliberate
to pleasure, perfected

I don't imagine
how you just might
prove every thrust, how
your whole soul would open
envelop the fullness of me
I don't envision watching
the arch of your spine
lift up from sheet
twisted in fevered grasp
how I might close my eyes
feel your hips rise and

rock with me
into every swerve
lean your every curve
fully intent
into this kiss
I taste this rush of lust
as you give in wet
to the nature
of we

I don't wonder
how I would read
pictures your nails paint
on the cave walls
of my back
drawn in response
to every question my fingers
ever asked of your ribs,
whispered from the peak
of lifted tips
on the canvas where I traced you
chased you into places

you've never been
I don't wonder
how the pulse of your stomach
would twitch and glisten
how I'd listen
to your entirety
screaming soul secrets
your mouth can only mime
to heaven, in wide open silence

to stand back
watch you dance
lost in the throes
of hopeless delight
then to start again from this angle
moments I once only craved

no I don't dream
not of reality
instead
every day
I wake you up
to live my fantasy

One Day, Perhaps, to Plant Again

I used to watch the news thankful
that I did not live in a war torn nation
where my survival would likely depend on
how well-hidden I could remain
moving from building crumbles
to building burnt out crouching soft

so very aware of the raging doom
waging war on all things beautiful

over-dusted hummingbird
caked in ash and the thick char of destruction

flitting so delicate from broken pistil
stem and seed

so very aware of the raging doom
waging war on all things beautiful

Push and Pull

I walk a fine line
of spoken word
poet spitting hot fire
and crafter of noble things
who drip honey from
sterling silver tongued spoon

she walked the fine line
of "oh, I'm just a fan
can you say something pretty?"
and "Can you take me?
Make me the next poem
you can't help but dream into existence?"

#2 Pencil Skirt

she likes it when I look
          how could I not?

caught up on a hot day
          she's   frozen scoops
dropped on a hot plate

left in the hot sun
          chocolate lingers
how could she not run
          across my fingers and

          drip from the tips
I can almost taste her liplocks
          and tongue grips

her deepest melanin
          a felon when I fell in hers
just might   steal a kiss like
          this?   yeah   it's mine

when her hips grind on my mind

ankles cross on my spine

when I worship at her inner temple

when her inner thighs compress and caress my jawline

pyramids fall and we can stop time

she likes it when I look

so I hold her gaze in a simple embrace

just enough to get started

her spark is erotic yet guarded

I can't see it but I know it's

wet parted

she likes it when I look

so I try and pretend like I don't notice

like I won't focus on a

number two pencil skirt take note this

sub-Saharan feline meanwhile

my stream of consciousness

makes a beeline

wondering just how tight   how high the rise
    would it rip or slip up over your thighs

she likes it when I look

I know the roll of her eyes
    by heart   by now
    I'm well acquainted   with
every quiver
subtle shiver
tap into her inner vision

wishing already I could see her
    again
when she turns in stride
    looks back to say:

    watch my ass   as I walk away
she

likes it   when I look

damn…

Local Eric Translation

28 But let a man examine himself, and so let him eat of the bread
and drink of the cup. 29 For he who eats and drinks in an unworthy
manner, eats and drinks judgement unto himself, not discerning
carbs and high caloric intake of bread and wine. 30 For this reason
many are weak among you, and many sleep. 31 And Jesus said unto
the disciples, This is going to go straight to my thighs. Ugh *

1 Corinthians 11:28-31 (L E T)

*contains some shit from the king james bible

These&esohT

hey teacher
WHAT ARE THOOOOOOSE?

oh these? no it's cool I'm happy to oblige you
this is FUBU   for us   not by you

yeah you got me now let me try you

you know how your mom likes to shop at the
mexican market?
or when your car breaks down
don't she race around town
find a latino shop to park it?

well that's community
unified use   of your   loose currency
to stimulate build   and produce currency
that's how you boost your local economy

but
instead of sharing the wealth   recycle that   dollar we
preparing ourselves   for the cycle of   black poverty
it's a shame   cuz we once had   sovereignty

black business reigned supreme until they came screaming
rained demon fire from on high
then   consistent with his story
rewrote this story
whitewashed how those black halls treated me   and
I don't trust the White House   but

that's just the Black Wall Street in me

so I say we rebuild it
that's what these footfalls mean to me

but you can buy clothes   Rolex and Rolls
I'll spend my soul on this black man's soles

because every time I buy black
I buy back
into us   and trust when I say
I feel no shame to rock a name no one sees

as you kick rocks   look down at your feet
ask yourself
well damn   what are *THESE?*

Tragic Kiss

he floats into my garden
returned drawn
visions of beauty spur him on
he glides silently effortless
over a sea of bright crimson
my bed of roses

under a warm golden sun
pausing at each in search of one

though highly visible he knows only the scent
it's deep violet hue majestically stands
out of place yet serene
at peace

lighting on the delicate flower he inhales deeply
the orchid bends 'neath his weighted touch

a gust from the corners where the four winds blow
the roses give shudder
releasing petals fluttered
scattered to cover the rich black soil

the violet by breeze is bowed upon these
crimson leaves for which I toil

and over a dead sea of bright red
my brand new bed of rose petals
he drinks

Just Black Enough

I just wanted to ball and I did even after your laughter
when I turned and heard the words to the theme song to Shaft, I
still didn't react like I could

why make you think what you did was okay
just to save face when you called out my race
by me acting like you thought I would

but even when you were long gone
and the points I scored no longer meant
anything more than the games I won
my mind was still on the nights events

so halted at a red signal searchin' how I feel
when a black and white off to my left
catches sight, puts his bright through my windshield

interruption of my reflection dramatic turn in the
intersection in my direction?

I smile maybe he don't like my style.
or is it just my profile

I know what I'll do I won't wait for the red and blue

I see green and pull through the light
pull to the right hands in plain sight

is there a problem officer?
no, I'm alone.
the gym, on my way home.
a black Honda, or ride like mine?
nah, things on my mind I'm not looking at cars.
yeah. You have a good night too.

on my way back to my home

kinda funny how I find it
in my neighborhood, my car
it's always nice to be reminded
just how black you really are

#2 Pencil Skirt #2

you must like it when I look
how could you not?

I see you at the store
in pajama bottoms and a tank top
curlers and a plastic bag
with a carefully applied base of
"fuck you, say sum'n" brand concealer on your face, the righteous
flame in your 3rd eye long gone out,
reduced to shadows Smoldering and smoking,
preemptively choking the breath from me

I see you standing in the street
yelling at a stranger over what was   probably nothing at all
little girls stand tall, off to the side
too young to be sour Sponge
but absorbing your tone and stance
to take and practice alone
in the mirror, at home, then prance
around school, new skills on display, teaching young boys a game
they never wanted to play

I see you
declare to the world you don't need no man while at the same time
claiming to be queen
but I see you demean your seed and I feel for young king
stop and think, what if you're slowly killing the Spirit of the next
dr. king?

I see you
posting video clips inviting men to watch your ass shake and drool
over your chocolate fault-line flimsy fabric ass quake

yes, your body is thick and you accomplish the amazing
simply maintaining your pride when, in these days, industry plays
        Upon your natural insecurities   trying to find
ways to weigh you down make you frown over what you weigh

truth is,
we prefer the sexy swerve of Natural curvy any day

but it's not a good look, when
I see you choosing to express your perfectly free mind with,
"Dear Instagram, Bless-me-help-me-take-this-selfie, ass-first-that-
all-the-men-may-see-and-make-me-tap-tap-wealthy"
and it's not healthy that you don't even make me ask first

so yeah...
I might look for a couple seconds
maybe even come back for seconds...

allow me to offer some perspective:
if you can't help but lead with your best Quality then don't expect
me to see you from any other perspective

but I get it
you just want me to acknowledge you So I try and pretend like I
don't notice this ignorant trend that just won't die
she doesn't believe she could ever be a world star
so she goes to WorldStar to browse and post fights

yes, you are "real" and quite possibly about that life
but black WOMEN have real struggles
so why not share that fight?
you SEE the strength of black men
and desire to fit in by adopting a role for which you were not
meant

allow me to offer some perspective
your strength is not in the swing of your fist
but in your healing kiss

your strength is durability   is righteous indignation
your strength is ingenuity, and in the face of adversity,
                                                            patience
your strength is strength itself

but I get it
you just want me to respect you   so I see you
                    I see your heart   I see your fear
                    I see your frustration   I see your pain
so I understand why She likes it when I look
because my presence is comfort and my energy brings balance

she likes it when I look
she needs me to look
she needs me   and   I *see* you

so...
be more than black woman
                    be mother
                    be   queen
                    be   earth
but, please
just be better than what I see

#2 pencil skirt #2

B r a i n S t o r m

the air still with anticipation the sky hanging low
o m i n o u s g r a y c l o u d s extend overhead
e m i t m ena c i n g r u m bl e s

electrical currents course through the moisture
threatening to gather and strike
the wind is almost non existent
as if hiding from the impending rage
on the brink of which is nature

I almost miss the flash of light
the crack is coming but whe…

the deafening roar is shocking
one two fifty drops suddenly a
b i ll i o n g a l l o ns
of water are released in
torrential downpour

my mind is flooded
I've got an
idea…

RANDOM THOUGHT

"Not all cops..."

Great. I totally agree.
Now let's get back to the ones who do, who are.

If we were talking about teachers who molest students, then no one would be focused on reminding the public that "all teachers aren't bad." There would be no extra effort to make the public feel safe through public relations stunts, like teachers walking through the city with signs that say Free Hugs or Hug a Teacher, all the while, followed by a camera. Think about that: if I film myself every time I give money to charity, or buy meals for homeless people, and posted it to social media, wouldn't you start to question my motives? Should I start posting my everyday activities to show that "all black men aren't bad?" No. That would be ridiculous.

We point out the bad because it is against the norm, the good. We point it out so it can be fixed. Pointing out the good when so much is wrong, when the stakes are so high, is borderline offensive. This is no time for sandwiching constructive criticism:

"So, you show up to your shift on time every day, and that's great! Now, you did kill two unarmed people last month, so there's room for improvement there...but your uniform is always neatly pressed! And your paperwork has relatively few typos...of course, conflicting accounts with eyewitnesses...but hey, your marksmanship is superb!" Obviously, taking someone's life is the worst thing one can do. It cannot be fixed later when you learn, "Oops, we arrested the right guy over here. I meant to tell you...you just shot the wrong man."

But it puts things into perspective when you think about your own kids and the teachers who have daily access to them. You wouldn't feel the need to defend all the good teachers. Your focus would be solely on removing and prosecuting the guilty parties.

And all of the good teachers would simply go on doing their jobs well. And most importantly, if they knew what another teacher was up to, they'd report it. Because good teachers put the safety and well-being of the students over their friendships and loyalty to the teachers' union.

But for some reason, people choose to point out the cops that do their job, as though it is an appropriate response to highlighting those who actually don't.

No reasonable person thinks all cops are bad. Not even me.

Not all cops...

Not all thugs...

Not all black...

Not all white...

Not all people...

Because to generalize about anything is often going to be untrue.

(Although, *not all generalizations are bad...*)

The Beauty of Dragons

or

Flowers | Bears | Candles

or

Pretty Things

To all the best parts of me

Rosalie Kira Mikele

I don't know that you will be a girly girl
covered in bows and frills and all things pink
but I know I will treat you like a princess
every day Shower you with love and
affection Court you with flowers from
the moment you can understand
how similar is a rose to your name
how precious are you both

how equally delicate your
heart to velvet petals
not to be peeled
and plucked
but protected
allowed to flourish
a treasure to be admired

your hypoallergenic pillow
will be covered with plush bears,
your favorite teddy pulled close
while you sleep Sharing your heartbeat
because
the only thing you know about this world is
the steady pulse of mommy's chest calms you
and the strength of daddy's hands and voice
soothe your soul While you sleep
dreaming of pretty things

I will teach you how to recognize a man who loves you
and I'm sure I will struggle with finding a balance between
giving you pretty things and showing you what it really means
to be adored Lavish you with gifts

knowing I could never repay the gift you are

I will also have to teach you the beauty of dragons
that roses have thorns   And the fluffiest puppy
conceals needle -point teeth   in good intentions
they come disguised Sometimes pretty things hurt
sometimes   pretty things are dragon wings
shimmery and gossamer
in flight   Beating soft
against the endless blue
so you never see the flaming cauldron
roiling in the belly   set to pass over
sickle and scythe Rows of terrible teeth
baby some men will come as dragons
on beating wings   A beautiful death
who mask pungent decay in custom cologne

might remind you   of candles
smoky mesquite and sandalwood
charm   a hint of vanilla Just might take you back to
flickering lights on stormy nights Power out
so daddy made games over candlelit dinner

scruffy neck beard hugs
tickled you to laughter's poem
Danced his hands across the ceiling
just for you   To soothe your soul
just so you wouldn't be afraid of the dark

but I need you to understand
that the shadow within the heart of man   is the only darkness
that daddy fears

for you

on my way to work   I saw
a man standing on the sidewalk
staring   at a Memorial pile   of
flowers   bears   and   candles

and I prayed I never live to regret
bringing   you   my pretty thing
into a world equal parts
Beauty   and pain

Local Eric Translation

3 And when the morrow had fully come, Jesus spake unto the
disciples saying, 4 "Thou hast eaten tacos, but verily I say unto thee;
this day shalt thou eat lemon pepper, and garlic Parmesan shall rest
upon thine chin." 5 And there was much weeping and gnashing of
teeth because that Wingstop had departed from their midst, and no
longer dwelt in the city.

After the Cubs Won the World Series

when the Cubs won their first World Series in 108 years
I was unmoved

amid men and women falling into each other's arms
in sobbing release decades of frustration washed away in a single
moment of realization

generations had been born, lived, and died
without a glimpse of what
they could only hope to see

and suddenly Hope was made manifest
a tangible reminder of promises kept

and I, unmoved
declared it just a game

and wondered where do raw unfettered emotion hide
how they lie dormant when lives are in the balance

How to Write a List Poem

one: walk into the bathroom and notice there is no tissue.

no, **ONE**: buy tissue OFTEN

two: stockpile

wait

one: find out what gives you the emergency poops

two: don't eat that shit

actually

one: don't watch counting poems, you don't want to be influenced

by popular trends and fads

hold on

one: go to kindergarten and learn to count. At least to five, but sometimes as high as 20, although by that point, you're probably rambling about a subject that, no doubt, has some sort of mass appeal, since after all, we are all creatures of the same basic experience, but 20 points is likely to be well over 4 or five minutes - depending on how fast you speak, but of course, you do want the listener to hear and retain more than just the numbers, and really the list poem has been done to death

so

one: be extremely creative with yours, should you decide to write a list poem

or better yet

one: don't write one

Ten Easy Steps for Being Impatient

1. crave juice
2. pull into supermarket lot
3. park car
4. walk into store
5. assess long ass lines
6. perform cost-benefit analysis
7. return to car
8. go home
9. drink water
10. pretend it's juice from a clear fruit

13 Words I Have Grown Weary of Hearing

Black

Boy

Body

Always

Feared

Unarmed

Ground

Never

Still

Enough

Death

Justified

Again

Questions for Kaepernick

who do you think you are golden son of Ra?

who, you natural
carbon crown stretching out for
melanin moons?

who do you think you are
you peaceful sword in righteous flame?

is your enlightenment salvation?

do you tread across battle-worn
steps traversed well by great men?

where are the throngs pressing at your back
surging onward?

will they ever hear you
in silent protest necessity born?

do you hear the bell?
will you pay the toll?

my earthen vessel | burnt brass cast
your meat casing | well done
my god | element
your fucking | nigger
my what lies beneath | the white sheet
your four hour | open display
my afro | stand
your cut it off | pink slip
my love | me
your lynch | him
my by any means | necessary
your german shepherd | fire hose
my panther party | breakfast program
your freeze and also | show me your hands
my melanin | deep
your stand | your ground
my heavenly | home
your go back | to africa
my here | present
your broken | level glare
my life is | direct threat
your always | threatened
my only | life
your it's only | black

That is to Say,
My Body | Black

Flip the Girl and Her Chair

how should I take it when you proceed beyond
conventional intentions of behavior interventions

how should I take your elevated heart rate escalated

my world tilts and dangles
strangely close to the precipice
at dangerous angles
my throat prisoner
who could envision your strangles
would go so unappreciated
as overreactions go
I am grossly underwhelmed

words I wrote, thoughts I spoke
rules I broke
brought down on my head

and all I ever said was

"No..."

|Noah's| Park|

we have learned each to love
our captivity born free| least
of all mentally| we settle for
zoo| no clue the view is
intentionally deceptive| need
build our own preserve| can't
go back to
motherland| connect to
motherland in us| based on
images fed as chum| so we
slip on slurry buckets sloppy
overflow| when god tells
Noah bring two of
each| black man woman
become traveling zoo| animal
park| get used to bars| don't
know gods voice but help
build the ship ourselves| then
separate into careful
subgenus| and as animals we
warden our very own cages|

When Nouns Become Verbs

[video]

as an active young boy back before back knees and joints were of more concern than scoring points we used to say things like JORDAN!!! with that fadeaway or jumping to catch a touchdown pass over the head of my defender I Randy Moss the highest man and then of course Heisman

we followed examples of the physically gifted who'd seemingly ascended to a higher plane of existence a realm above we believed what we'd seen on tv and thought we could

Be Like Mike

I turned my attention to music

no pain too heavy for Coltrane Rollins and Parker entirely illuminated the darker corners of my entirety

and on any given day you might find me spinning in a random mirror trying to *remember the time*

I believed what I'd seen on tv and thought I could

Be...like...Mike

see, when Nouns become Verbs
when names come to mean action They can reflect the time
and redefine the nature of our very being and

when that persona becomes more prevalent and less relevant words
subside in defeat I can't help but wonder
how long until our names become verbs for dying in the street?

when will the world understand it?
rather than accept the fate we've been handed That justice isn't
black and white, but shades of Freddy Grey
who got *Sandy Blanded?*
I Say Her Name in honor
but it bothers me that yet another man of *sandy* complexion
will escalate a simple situation simply because the
bold, brilliant, vibrant, vivid spirit of my people could never be so
bland as to suit his simple taste Never enough kind words to *sand*
down the rough edges of a gruff exterior

sandy…bland   Beautiful queen may she forever rest
but her life   was the Antithesis   of the picture
her very name suggests   And yet

another family told
    don't fret he in a better place But
no conversation can explain it away   And
no compensation can return Freddie Grey from the ether
    or *John Crawford* either

only 22 Not even holding a 22   but only his big homie knows how much he'd grown in those 22 So who knows what the next two decades might have decided? The
children for whom he might have provided?   The
cases over which he might have presided?

Justice John Crawford

we march for progress   hoping for leaps and bounds
only to watch justice john-*crawl forward*
Mortally wounded

so we broken verbs traverse stages with spoken words for all ages huddled masses yearning to breathe free   we

choke out lies
strangle hate
speak TRUTH to power
Eric Garner support

so that one day   when we decide to stop playing
12 years a slave
we can Tamir rise up   as one people unified
abandon the insanity and fight for our place in humanity
Hands up   demand that this beautiful hue
this skin Micheal *Browned* by the sun   be as respected, as the
celestial body we've reflected from day one

but until then, we will continue to share these words
and hope our little nouns will never become verbs
who believe what they see on tv and grow up and

Be   like   Mike

B ackSl id er II

spend your whole life wise
holy straight
narrow
and godly

didn't know thine eye w's
only aimed at
sparrows
and not me
god, he
got me
with Agape

We, Who Chase Away the Rising Sun

we leap from strata

slash

at a

slow-churned sky

biting vicious

the golden glow

lest he bring with him

yet another

M o n d a y

grim

Local Eric Translation

8 Oh taste and see that the Lord is good; 9 kinda spicy...a little
citrus for balance. 10 Lovely plating. *

Psalm 34:8 (L E T)

*contains some shit from the king james bible

appendix

glossary

aggressive – adj. see, black male p.56

agape – n. (uh-GAW-pee) unconditional love which certain churches teach god has for mankind. Except for those whom he aggressively murdered with a flood. Or fire. Or pillars of salt. Or plague. p.102

apostolic – n. a "holiness" christian faith, branch of pentacostal, largely based on salvation as described in acts p.22

backslider – n. aggressive term used by select church members to describe irrational actions by former believers (ie studying outside the bible to determine origin or verity by means of thorough research) p.54

beauty
bold – adj. a description of contrasting color, the diverse collection of differently shaded persons inhabiting a given area or region p.14

dgaf – v. 1. the inability to care about a given matter
2. aggressive antipathy
3. don't give a fuck p.36

flip the girl – v. an entirely improper yet over-defended irrationally aggressive response to any defiant student of color for any reason p.96

is – n. is p.10

justice john-crawl forward – v. 1. evasive action taken by a man attempting to escape his own murder
2. the pace at which justice moves for people of color p.100

kaepernick – n. 1. colin
2. fearless nfl quarterback
3. defiance in the tradition of muhammad ali and jim brown p.94

lies – n. see united states, government p.19, 50

locs – n. a spiritually infused naturally occurring kink, often seen as too aggressive an appearance for corporate workplace (own your own business) p.23

metaphor food – n. that which poets aggressively serve to those who, unaware they were even hungry, trudge onward. p.11

michael brown – v. the process by which the sun or an eternal creative force imbues one with an abundance of melanin, causing some to see the carrier as inherently aggressive, beastly, irrational, and impervious to any less than 10 bullets p.101

monday grim – n. the sober and wholly numbing expectation that the latest unarmed victim of police aggression will not be the last p.103

sandy blanded – v. 1. what happens to proud black women, whose innate royalty being perceived as aggressive, does not allow them to leave prison alive, under mysterious circumstances 2. to die suspiciously while in police custody p.99

sum'n – n. "something" when you don't give enough fucks to bother with enunciation (see, stolen culture, see also "fuck your language, I want mine back") p.76

supple slow – n. a curve or line readily positioned for carnal bliss p.61

w's – v. was, abbreviated for lyricality p.102

video and audio links

(to scan: the author recommends you download a

QR CODE READER

from the app store or google play)

In Which I Do Not Apologize to the Roach for the Spray

p.14

Weapons of Warfare

p.26

After America Determines Beyoncé to be Black and Kendrick Lamar Too Much Out Loud

p.27

video credit: Pearl Yanez

Happy Lies: The Married Woman

p.40

“…aggressive”

p.56

video credit: Michael Thomas Cooper

When Nouns Become Verbs/Be Like Mike

p.98

video credit: Larry Ealy

Legalese:

Lawyers and Politicians

I cannot, in all good faith, and with no uncertainty, say that I deny the falseness of any said inaccuracies – perceived or otherwise – contained within the collective aforementioned statements; the verity of which, I would not purport to dispute.

12 Things You Don't Know About Me

12) I have two phobias: becoming a paraplegic, and being stranded in the ocean.

11) I was born in Texas.

10) I wrote my first love song because I was mad at my mom and wanted to manipulate her into feeling guilty.

9) I've never been on a train.

8) The only time I've been high was 20 minutes before youth choir rehearsal.

7) The week after 9/11, I broke my ankle

6) Prior to teaching elementary P.E., I didn't like kids. At...all.

5) If time travel ever becomes possible, I will go to every length to avoid 10yr old me. That little fucker was annoying.

4) ...is my favorite number.

3) When I was a kid, I thought jazz meant Kenny G. Then I learned about Charlie Parker, Ella Fitzgerald, and Thelonious Monk.

2) I have, at different points in my life, wanted to be S.W.A.T. and a super villain.

1) I'm not nearly as clever as I think I am.

Special thanks to Samuel Rain, without whom I may never have had the courage to see this through to completion. I appreciate you, sir!

My deepest appreciation and sincere thanks to Nikia Chaney for your guidance and the consideration you have shown me. And to Romaine Washington, for adding your wonderful words, I am so very grateful!

Thanks for playing along, folks. I hope you've enjoyed this as much as I have. Be on lookout for my next project, dedicated to my newborn daughter:

The Beauty of Dragons

Image by: Eric DeVaughnn

About the author: Eric DeVaughnn is a writer, poet, and spoken word artist on a quest to uncover honesty in art. At an early age, he developed an almost reverent appreciation for all things creative. His mission is to seek and express truth, and to uphold the standard of excellence established well before him. He has been a featured reader and guest performer on many diverse stages and venues United States.

Ever the proponent for critical thinking and challenging perception, Eric uses wordplay and storytelling to examine the higher truths of life under the moniker "Thought Requires Uncommon Effort," or simply :

T . R . U . E

www.ingramcontent.com/pod-product-compliance
Lightning Source LLC
LaVergne TN
LVHW051006080826
845145LV00009B/2491

* 9 7 8 0 9 9 9 6 0 1 8 2 2 *